©Published by Peter Haddock Limited,
Bridlington, England.

Printed in U.A.E.

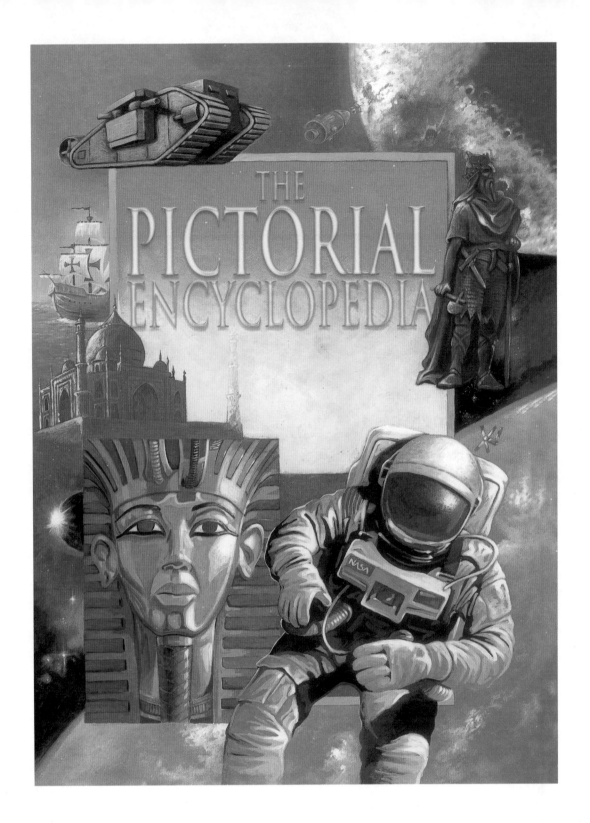

THE PICTORIAL ENCYCLOPEDIA

PETER HADDOCK PUBLISHING

CONTENTS

Frontispiece: Joan of Arc   (page 73)

Chapter One
AROUND THE WORLD

Everywhere in the world interesting subjects abound. For instance why was the towering Monument in London erected? Who built the Taj Mahal and why? Why is the home of the President of the United States called "The White House"? Which country built and gave the Statue of Liberty to the United States? Did King Arthur rid St Michael's Mount of a giant who was killing the cattle on the mainland? These questions and many more are answered in the following pages.

St Michael's Mount

This huge, granite rock is off the Cornish coast of England, near the town of Marazion. It is crowned by a stately home that was once a castle. At high tide the Mount is surrounded by deep water. When the tide is out people can walk to the rock from the mainland on a raised path called a causeway.

It is said that once a one-eyed giant lived on the island. At low tide he would cross to the mainland and kill the cattle. King Arthur finally tackled the giant and killed him.

The Royal Pavilion

George, Prince of Wales, son of King George III, wanted a home at Brighton, Sussex. He bought himself an old farmhouse and hired John Nash, a famous architect, to transform it into the truly splendid building that can be seen today.

In 1850 Queen Victoria sold the Royal Pavilion to Brighton.

Then in 1982, after many years of neglect, restoration of the structure and stonework was begun. It took ten years to complete.

Tourists visiting the Royal Pavilion are enchanted not only because of its striking Eastern exterior but also with the beauty of its interior and the gardens.

It is said that the ghost of Prince George was once seen walking along one of the underground passages of the Pavilion.

Glastonbury Abbey

At Glastonbury in Somerset stand the ruins of an ancient abbey. It is said that on the site the first Christian church in England was built.

Among the ruins, the Abbot's Barn is still intact. It is six hundred years old. The abbey's kitchens also remain and are now a museum.

In legend, King Arthur of Round Table fame was buried there.

Glenfinnan

On the Road to the Isles in the Western Highlands of Scotland is Glenfinnan and there stands a tall column surmounted by the statue of a kilted Highlander.

It was here on August 19th 1745 that a banner was unfurled by Prince Charles Edward Stuart, or Bonnie Prince Charlie as he is better known (see page 85).

Charles had taken a ship from France and landed in Scotland with only a few friends. Now he was calling the Scottish clansmen to support him in his bid for the throne of Britain. He was soon joined by thousands of brave Scotsmen but their rebellion finally ended in tragedy and defeat at the Battle of Culloden in 1746.

Edinburgh

The capital city of Scotland is Edinburgh. The city was named Edwin's Burgh after King Edwin of Northumbria who reigned between AD 617 and AD 633. It was King Edwin who either built or enlarged the castle which was built on what is now called Castle Rock. The city grew up around the castle.

Tourists flock to Princes Street where there are many splendid shops and where stands the huge monument to Sir Walter Scott, Scotland's most famous author (above).

Taj Mahal

In India there stands one of the most beautiful buildings in the world. It was built by the Mogul Emperor, Shah Jehan, near Agra three hundred and fifty years ago.

It is in fact a magnificent tomb of white marble, exquisite in shape and proportion, and set in a splendid garden, quiet and peaceful.

In India in those days women held a very lowly place but Mumtaz Mahal was the powerful and favourite wife of Shah Jehan who was responsible for many conquests.

She was constantly at his side no matter what the undertaking.

She was with him on one of his campaigns when she died. He was inconsolable and it seemed as though the light of his life had gone out. At enormous cost he gathered together the choicest of materials and the most skilful workmen to erect a tomb of lasting wonder.

Twentieth-century pollution, as a result of so many visitors, has sadly caused the building to deteriorate.

Timor

The island of Timor lies north of Australia and is the most easterly of the Lesser Sundas Islands. Timor covers nearly thirty-one thousand square kilometres and is an important cattle-rearing area. Until 1975 the eastern part of the island was independent, when it was taken over by Indonesia. Many Timorese resent being part of Indonesia and campaign for independence.

The traditional homes of the Timorese are built on stilts to stop vermin entering and infesting the rooms.

Tokyo

The capital city of Japan is Tokyo and, with a population of about twelve million, it is one of the most densely populated cities in the world. It is situated on the island of Honshu and stands on both banks of the River Sumida.

Tokyo is divided into wards and in the centre of Kojimachi ward is the palace of the Emperor. It dates from 1888.

At one time, the city was known as Jeddo or Yedo but it was given the name Tokyo which means "Eastern Capital" in 1868.

There are many temples in Tokyo and a number of theatres. Two of the main theatres are the Kabukiza Theatre (left) and the Nippon Theatre.

Mexico City

Mexico City is the capital of Mexico. It stands at a height of two thousand three hundred and eighty metres above sea level. Mexico was founded by Hernando Cortez in 1522.

Below is the Zocalo which is a very spacious square from which run the main streets of the city. Behind the Zocalo is the cathedral. It is one of the largest cathedrals on the continent of America.

The Mermaid of Copenhagen

Eiffel Tower

One of the most famous sights in Paris, capital of France, is the Eiffel Tower. It is over four hundred metres tall and made entirely of iron and steel. It was built in 1889 as part of an exhibition held in the city.

The Tower was intended to be a temporary structure for the exhibition but it was so popular that it has remained. A lift carries visitors to the top of the Tower from where views of the city can be seen. It is named after Gustave Eiffel, the man who designed it.

Overlooking the harbour of Copenhagen, capital of Denmark, is a small statue of a beautiful girl. The statue is a tribute to the memory of Denmark's greatest writer, Hans Christian Andersen.

Andersen was born in the small town of Odense in 1805 to a poor family. At the age of fourteen Hans Andersen left school and went to Copenhagen to become an actor.

Ten years later he gave up the stage to write. His early books were serious novels, but in 1835 he produced a collection of fairy tales. The book was enormously popular.

One of the stories was about the little mermaid who fell in love with a prince and wanted to leave her life in the sea to live with him. After Andersen's death in 1875 the citizens of Copenhagen erected the statue of the little mermaid to honour him. The story was made into a film by Walt Disney in 1933.

Azay-le-Rideau

France is renowned for its splendid castle-type homes called *chateaux*. Among them one of the finest is Azay-le-Rideau.

It stands surrounded by weeping willows at the side of the Indre River. The chateau has been said to look like a fairy palace. It has been owned by the French Government since 1905.

Kracow

In the fourteenth century, Kracow became the capital of Poland. It remained so until 1595 when Warsaw became the capital.

In the Second World War, Poland was occupied by Germany and Russia. Today it is an independent country. One of Kracow's most picturesque buildings is the Stanislaus Cathedral (right). The city stands on the Vistula, the most important river in Poland.

The Tower of London

Beside the River Thames stands the ancient Tower of London. It is the oldest fortress, palace and prison in Europe.

Not long after the Norman Conquest of 1066, William the Conqueror started to build the White Tower (above). Later kings have added more buildings and towers. The moat was made wider and deeper during the reign of King Richard the Lionheart.

Tourists from all over the world flock to the Tower of London, not only to see the old fortress but particularly to see the Crown Jewels which have been kept there for hundreds of years.

In the olden days kings and queens lived in the Tower before they were crowned. They would set out in great processions to be crowned at Westminster Abbey.

Many famous people were imprisoned in the Tower, amongst them Queens Anne Boleyn, Catherine Howard and Queen Elizabeth I, before she became queen.

St Paul's Cathedral

This magnificent building was designed by the famous architect, Sir Christopher Wren. It was built to replace the medieval church that was destroyed in 1666 during the Great Fire of London.

Its great dome is famous all over the world. In fact, Wren based it on Michelangelo's design for St Peter's in Rome which is the world's largest church.

It was not until 1675 that the building of the new cathedral was started. A tax on all the coal brought to London was specially raised to pay for the new building. The first stone was laid on June 21st 1675. Wren worked for thirty-five years on his masterpiece. He was knighted in 1672. When he died in 1723 he was buried in the Cathedral.

Many famous people and heroes of Britain are buried in St Paul's. Among the most famous are Admiral Horatio Nelson and the first Duke of Wellington.

The Monument

This column, which stands sixty-two metres high, is at Pudding Lane in the City of London. It was erected by Sir Christopher Wren to commemorate the Great Fire of London. The height of the Monument is the exact distance from its foot to the baker's shop in Pudding Lane near London Bridge where the fire actually began at two o'clock in the morning of September 2nd 1666.

The summer had been hot and dry. The fire spread rapidly for a brisk wind was blowing. House after house caught fire and the flames headed towards the river where piles of goods were soon blazing.

The fire raged for five days and only stopped when the wind changed direction. Fire-fighting equipment was scarce so there was little chance of putting out the fire. In all the Great Fire destroyed thirteen thousand houses and eighty-seven churches on four hundred streets.

It was claimed at the time that only eight people died in the flames.

Caernarvon

This town stands on the north-west coast of Wales and is famous for its magnificent castle.

The warrior king, Edward I, started to build the castle in 1283 and it was completed in 1328. At this time Edward was fighting to impose his rule on Wales. His eldest son was born there in 1284 and Edward offered him to the Welsh people to be their own Prince of Wales. Since then the eldest son of the reigning monarch has always been given the title of Prince of Wales. The investiture of the present Prince of Wales took place at Caernarvon Castle in 1969.

Pembroke Castle

After the Norman Conquest of 1066, the noblemen who came with Duke William the Conqueror built castles in order to control the local inhabitants.

The great, stone castle of Pembroke in south-west Wales was begun by Gerald de Winter, a Norman knight.

The site was chosen for its strong, natural defences formed by the tidal Pembroke River. The huge keep with its two-metre thick walls was raised at the beginning of the thirteenth century.

During the Middle Ages, England and Wales were often at war although Pembroke Castle always remained in the hands of the English.

One of the most famous people who lived in the castle was Henry Tudor who, it is said, was born there in 1456 in a room on the first floor of the gatehouse (right).

In 1485 he defeated King Richard III and replaced him on the throne of England as King Henry VII.

During the Civil War it was besieged by Oliver Cromwell and, after he captured it,

gunpowder charges were exploded against most of the towers and the gatehouse. Restoration did not begin until 1928. Today the castle attracts many visitors.

River Danube

This river is the most important in southern Europe. It rises in the Black Forest, south of Stuttgart, Germany, and flows for some eighteen hundred miles to the Black Sea.

The cities of Vienna, Budapest and Belgrade stand on the Danube. The famous waltz of Johann Strauss, the Viennese composer, is 'The Blue Danube".

Moscow

This is the capital city of Russia and it lies on the River Moskva.

The city was begun in 1156 when Prince Yuri Dolgoruky built a fortress or kremlin. The Tsar Ivan the Terrible made Moscow his capital. Moscow remained the capital until 1712, when St Petersburg took the honour. However, the Communists who took power in 1918 returned the capital to Moscow.

At the heart of the city is the Kremlin. The original fortress has long vanished and has been replaced by a complex of palaces and offices which is now the seat of government. St Basil's Cathedral is one of the most famous buildings. In front of the Kremlin is Red Square, used for parades and celebrations. The outer city consists of vast housing estates which are home to over ten million people.

The Temples of Abu Simbel

Ancient Egypt had a great civilisation which produced massive temples and tombs for the Pharaohs, who ruled the land from 2900 BC to 30 BC. Among the most impressive temples are those at Abu Simbel in southern Egypt. They were built about 1240 BC by Pharaoh Rameses II and are decorated with statues of the Pharaoh. In the 1960s the temples had to be moved in pieces to higher land when their site was flooded by the building of the Aswan Dam.

Lhasa

The holy place and chief city of Tibet in south-west China is Lhasa. The city stands on a fertile plain but the plain is completely surrounded by barren hills.

Lhasa was the seat of the Dalai Lama, the spiritual head of the Tibetans. On the death of a Dalai Lama a child born at the time and day of his death becomes the next Dalai Lama. However, in 1959 the present head of the Tibetans had to go into exile when the Chinese entered Tibet.

The palace of the Dalai Lama was the Potala, (below). It was guarded with great

care and, until the twentieth century, no Dalai Lama was ever seen in public. The present Dalai Lama was enthroned on February 22nd 1940, when he was six years old. Today Lhasa is quite an important trade centre.

France had sent money and soldiers to help the American settlers. The Statue of Liberty was a gift to the United States from France. It was erected in New York Harbour in 1884.

During the nineteenth century, refugees, fleeing from poverty and persecution in the Old World, sailed to America and the Statue of Liberty seemed to be greeting them as they arrived in New York.

The White House

The White House is home to the President of the United States of America. It stands in large gardens in the middle of Washington, capital of the United States, in the District of Columbia.

The White House was begun in 1792 but in 1813 it was burnt by the British who were at war with the United States. It was quickly rebuilt and painted white to hide the smoke stains. In 1948 the interior was modernised by President Truman and it has remained largely unchanged since.

The building is open to the public and about a million people visit it each year. The White House is home to the President and is also used for grand, state occasions.

It is said that the White House has at times been haunted by the ghost of President Lincoln, who was murdered in a theatre in Washington in 1865.

The Statue of Liberty

This huge, copper statue stands on a tiny island in New York Harbour. It is forty-six metres high from the feet to the top of the torch and is mounted on a pedestal forty-seven metres high.

The statue is a woman dressed in classical robes. She is stepping to freedom from a broken chain which lies at her feet. In her upraised, right hand is a flaming torch.

A lift will take visitors to the top of the pedestal. Then a spiral flight of one hundred and sixty-eight steps leads up to the lady's head. It is possible for thirty people to stand in the head.

During the American War of Independence,

Chapter Two
WORLD LEADERS

Famous rulers have appeared all through history. Not all came from famous or royal families. Britain's great war-leader, Sir Winston Churchill, was the grandson of the Duke of Marlborough. The father of Abraham Lincoln, the famous president of the United States of America, was a desperately poor settler living in Kentucky. There were brave women such as Queen Boadicea of the Iceni, and clever empresses like Catherine the Great of Russia. The lives of all of them were packed with amazing events and all lived though exciting adventures.

Sir Winston Churchill

Winston Leonard Spencer Churchill was born in 1874. He began his career as a soldier and journalist but after being elected to Parliament in 1900 he devoted the rest of his life to being a politician.

He was in and out of high office until 1939 when the Second World War broke out. In 1940 he became Prime Minister.

He rallied the spirits of the British people after Germany's victories in Belgium, Holland and France. Powerfully, he ruled Britain until the end of the war. He died in 1965.

William the Conqueror

William, Duke of Normandy, gained his nickname of 'the Conqueror' by a stunning series of victories which made him one of the most powerful men in northern Europe.

William was born in 1027, son of Robert the Devil, Duke of Normandy. In 1035 his father died and many lords refused to accept the eight-year-old William as their ruler. A civil war broke out in Normandy between nobles loyal to William and those who wanted his cousin, Guy of Burgundy, to be Duke. Not until 1047 did William finally defeat his enemies to become master of all Normandy. In 1049 he went to war with the Count of Anjou and captured many of his lands.

But William's greatest conquest came in 1066. In January William's friend, King Edward of England, died. The English chose the powerful Harold Godwinson, to be their king. William was furious as he had been promised the throne and Harold had promised to help him.

William gathered a huge army but bad weather stopped his fleet from sailing for England until the autumn.

On October 14th William met Harold in battle just north of Hastings. For many hours the English infantry resisted the attacks of the Norman cavalry but, as dusk fell, Harold was killed and his army finally gave way. After the victory, William hurried to London where he was crowned king. However, it was several years before William crushed all resistance.

As king, William introduced the Norman feudal system to England and completely reorganised the way the kingdom was governed. He ordered that a list be made of every property and village in England. The result, the Domesday Book, still exists and provides valuable information on the time.

William was killed after falling from his horse during a war with the French in 1087.

Alexander the Great

Alexander the Great was one of the most famous generals ever. He became King of Macedonia, a small kingdom in the Balkans, in 336 BC when he was aged just twenty. His father, Philip, had fought for many years in an endeavour to secure control over the whole of Greece. At last he conquered Athens but was assassinated soon afterwards. Once Alexander took over he continued his father's efforts to unite the cities of Greece under the rule of Macedonia.

He then invaded the Persian Empire. At the Battle of Issus, in 333 BC, Alexander defeated Emperor Darius of Persia in a spectacular battle. Darius had an army many times larger than Alexander's but the Persians were defeated when Alexander led a charge of specially-trained, heavy cavalry. Two years later Alexander defeated Darius again at the Battle of Arbela and the Persian Empire collapsed.

Alexander went on to conquer Syria, Egypt, Babylon and all lands as far as the Indus river in northern India.

He began to organise his vast conquests into a single empire but, in 323 BC, aged just thirty-three, Alexander caught a fever and died. After his death the empire was shared out by his generals.

Thereafter there was no man great enough to spread European culture as far as India and nearly two thousand years passed before British and French ships ventured as far as that mighty continent.

Henry VIII

This King is famous not only because he was the eighth and last King Henry but also because he married six wives.

He was born in 1491, the son of King Henry VII who was the first King of England of the House of Tudor. When in 1509 he came to the throne, the Catholic Church was powerful in England. One of Henry's best friends was Cardinal Thomas Wolsey (seen above with King Henry outside Hampton Court Palace which the Cardinal had built and thought wise to give to the King).

King Henry wanted a son who could inherit the throne when he, the King, died. But the King's wife, Queen Catherine of Aragon, had only one child, a daughter. So Henry, already tired of Catherine, wished to divorce her so that he could marry again.

He ordered Cardinal Wolsey to arrange a divorce but this Wolsey failed to do.

Henry removed all power from the Cardinal and the Catholic religion in England and became the Supreme Head of the Church. Now he no longer had to ask for a divorce. He demanded and secured one and in 1533 married Anne Boleyn, hoping for a son. Instead the new Queen bore him a daughter who later became Queen Elizabeth I. In 1536 he had Queen Anne executed and married Lady Jane Seymour.

By Queen Jane he had the son he had longed for but Jane died in childbirth. Thereafter Henry married Princess Anne of Cleves, divorced her and married Lady Catherine Howard. As Anne Boleyn had been executed, so was Catherine and then Henry married his last Queen, Lady Catherine Parr.

The early period of his long reign of thirty-six years was marked with a war with France. There followed attempts to seize Scotland and Ireland but these were unsuccessful and his kingdom was left heavily in debt when Henry died in 1547.

Queen Victoria

Only one monarch reigned for sixty-four years in England. She was Queen Victoria whose father, Edward, Duke of Kent, was the younger brother of two Kings, George IV and William IV.

Queen Victoria was christened Alexandrina Victoria when she was born in 1819. She was only eighteen years of age when on June 20th 1837 King William IV died. The Archbishop of Canterbury and the Lord Chamberlain were taken by coach through the night from Windsor Castle to Kensington Palace, the home of the young Princess. She was fast asleep when they arrived but they gave orders that she was to be awakened and told her that she was now the ruler of the greatest empire in the world.

She was crowned on June 28th 1838. She was not yet married but two years earlier, in May 1836, she had met her future husband, Prince Albert of Saxe-Coburg-Gotha, when, with his father, he paid a visit to Kensington Palace.

They met again in October 1839 and the next month she let it be known that she had fallen deeply in love with Prince Albert and

intended to marry him. On February 10th 1840 Queen Victoria and Prince Albert were married in the Chapel Royal, St James's Palace, London. They lived very happily together for twenty-one years and had nine children.

One great event that happened while Prince Albert - now known as Prince Consort - was alive, was the Great Exhibition held in the "Crystal Palace" in Hyde Park. It was Prince Albert who had thought of this great, international exhibition which, it was hoped, would turn the eyes of the world upon the products and industries of Great Britain. There were protests about the exhibition being held in Hyde Park for it was thought that rogues and would-be rioters would gather there.

Queen Victoria, though, supported her husband and the Great Exhibition was opened by the Queen on May 1st 1851. It was a great success, making a profit of a quarter of a million pounds.

When Prince Albert died on December 14th 1861 the Queen was broken-hearted and mourned him for the rest of her long life. She died in 1901 and was buried beside her husband in Frogmore, Windsor.

Hannibal

Hannibal was one of the greatest generals of the ancient world who won many victories for his North African city of Carthage. Carthage was a bitter rival of Rome, then building an empire in southern Europe. In 219 BC war broke out.

Hannibal was in Spain where Carthage held large territories. He decided on an amazing plan of campaign, to march his army to Italy and attack Rome. Hannibal had to fight his way through southern France and through the wild passes of the Alps before he arrived in Italy in the autumn of 218 BC. The tribes of northern Italy rose in rebellion against Rome and joined Hannibal in his march on Rome.

In 216 BC Rome gathered the finest and largest army that it had ever put in the field. There were nearly one hundred thousand men in the army which marched to Cannae where Hannibal was camped with his forty-five thousand troops.

Despite being outnumbered, Hannibal attacked. By a brilliant tactic, Hannibal surrounded the Romans and sent his men in to win complete victory. It is thought that seventy thousand Romans were killed for the cost of just four thousand Carthaginians, a terrible defeat for the proud city of Rome.

Despite all his great successes, Hannibal had to retreat from Italy when a Roman fleet destroyed the Carthaginian navy. The ships were carrying all the supplies and food that Hannibal needed for the army to continue fighting. In 202 BC Carthage was forced to surrender.

Then in 183 BC Hannibal was threatened with capture by Roman troops but, defiant to the end, he committed suicide.

Tutankhamen

The teenage Egyptian Pharaoh, or king, Tutankhamen is best known because of the magnificent treasures found in his tomb in 1922. But he was a ruler who had real influence on Egyptian history.

Tutankhamen was a teenager when he became Pharaoh in 1358 BC. His father, Akhenaton, had abandoned the old gods and the old capital city. Tutankhamen almost immediately began to worship the traditional gods of Egypt and returned his court to the capital of Thebes. He began to restore the temples but died suddenly at the age of about eighteen in 1353 BC. He was followed by his uncle, who was soon ousted by Horemheb, a successful general.

Although Tutankhamen was buried in a small tomb for a Pharaoh, it was richly furnished. Egyptians believed that a dead Pharaoh took with him to the next life objects buried with him. Tutankhamen was buried with gilded beds, war chariots and masses of jewellery. One of the most famous objects was a mask made of solid gold which was placed over the head of the dead Pharaoh. The tomb was discovered in 1922. by the British archaeologist, Howard Carter, and the treasures are now on display in Cairo.

Richard I

King Richard I of England was called the Lionheart because of his courage in battle. The third son of Henry II, he was born in 1157 and came to the throne of England in 1189.

He at once prepared the Third Crusade. This was a Christian expedition to the Holy Land to recover Jerusalem from the grip of the Muslims under their Sultan, Saladin.

After defeating Saladin twice, Richard made a truce with the Sultan and never captured Jerusalem. Richard's departure from the Holy Land was caused by the plotting of his younger brother, John, who, in Richard's absence, tried to seize the throne for himself. Richard returned and took control of his kingdom. There followed years of warfare in France and elsewhere. He was laying siege to the castle of Chaluz in France in 1199 when he was mortally wounded.

Sitting Bull

Sitting Bull was a great leader of the Sioux nation in North America. He led them in several wars, but failed to free them from the American Government.

Sitting Bull was born in about 1831. As a young man he took part in several raids against neighbouring tribes and became famous as a daring leader.

By 1875 Sitting Bull was supreme chief of all the Sioux.

When the government of the United States ordered the Sioux to hand over all their land and go to live on a small reservation, Sitting Bull refused. He gathered his warriors together. When American troops under General Custer advanced, Sitting Bull attacked and wiped them out. However, new and larger armies were sent against the Sioux and in 1881 Sitting Bull surrendered. His people were sent to reservations and forced to give up their land. In 1890 the Sioux leader was shot by police after an argument.

Napoleon

Napoleon Bonaparte was born at Ajaccio on the island of Corsica on August 15th 1769. In 1784 he was made a cadet in the military school at Paris.

He first rose to prominence in 1793. An English fleet was anchored off Toulon and Napoleon, now an artillery officer, was mainly responsible for its withdrawal.

From then on, his career was meteoric. In 1802 he became First Consul for life and in 1804 first Emperor of the French.

There followed many years of warfare during which he defeated one country after another. However, in 1812, he invaded Russia. The Russians retreated, devastating the countryside as they did so. (This is the origin of the phrase '"scorched-earth" policy'.) The French were then overcome by the onset of the severe Russian winter, many dying of cold and starvation, and Napoleon was forced to abandon the struggle.

In 1814 he was forced to abdicate and spent some time in exile on the island of Elba before escaping and returning to a brief period of power in 1815. That was the year of the battle of Waterloo when Napoleon's reign was finally ended.

He was exiled again, this time to the island of St Helena, and died there in 1821.

Elizabeth I

Queen Elizabeth I ruled during a time of great religious troubles but she managed to avoid civil war and protected England from foreign invasions.

Born in 1533, the daughter of Henry VIII, Elizabeth was a Protestant. When her Catholic sister, Mary, became Queen, Elizabeth was sent from court to Hatfield House to live in retirement. When Mary died in 1558, Elizabeth returned to London and was crowned Queen. She at once stopped the religious persecutions and declared that Catholics and Protestants could worship as they pleased so long as they were loyal to England.

When King Philip of Spain tried to lead a Catholic invasion in 1588 he found that English Roman Catholics preferred to support Elizabeth.

King Philip's great Armada of warships was attacked and harried by the English fleet under the command of seamen like Lord Howard of Effingham, Sir Francis Drake and Sir John Hawkins. Raging storms completed the defeat and destruction of the Armada

During her reign, England enjoyed much prosperity and peace. In this peace there was a flowering of culture which produced many famous artists, writers and poets. When Elizabeth died in 1603 she left a united and wealthy kingdom to her successor, James of Scotland.

Catherine the Great

Catherine became Tsarina, or Empress, of Russia at the age of thirty-three and led the Russian people to achieve greatness.

Catherine was born Sophia, daughter of a minor German prince, but in 1744 she married Peter, heir to the Russian throne, and changed her name to the more Russian Catherine.

Catherine soon became very popular with the people as a result of her dedication to duty and hard work. Her husband, Tsar Peter, though, ignored his people in order to have fun. Catherine came to power when her husband was murdered by a group of army officers only a few months after becoming the Tsar.

Catherine dedicated her life to ruling Russia. She led several successful wars against the Turks and took much land from Poland.

When she died in 1796 she left Russia a proud and powerful nation.

Cleopatra

Cleopatra, born 69 BC, was the last ruler of an independent Egypt before it was conquered by the Roman Empire in 30 BC.

Cleopatra was the daughter of Ptolemy XIII, King of Egypt. Her father died in 51 BC and she and her brother, Ptolemy, ruled jointly.

When Ptolemy tried to have his sister murdered, Cleopatra fled to Julius Caesar for help. Caesar led an army to Egypt, defeated Ptolemy and made Cleopatra ruler.

By 41 BC the Roman Empire was divided between Octavian and Mark Antony. Cleopatra and Antony were in love and Antony began using his Roman soldiers to make Egypt more powerful. Eventually Octavian lost his patience and declared war on Antony and Cleopatra. After a long war Octavian was totally victorious. Cleopatra was captured. To escape being taken to Rome, she allowed a poisonous snake to bite her so that she could die with dignity in the Kingdom of Egypt.

Queen Boadicea

The Celtic queen, Boadicea or Boudicca, led a rebellion against the Roman rule of Britain in AD 62. She nearly succeeded but her final defeat meant death to thousands of her own people.

When King Prasutagus died in AD 62 he left his kingdom of the Iceni in East Anglia to Rome. But the Romans took not only the kingdom, but also the personal wealth of the royal family and noblemen.

Prasutagus's widow, Boadicea, was beaten and his two daughters cruelly misused. The Iceni were a proud tribe and refused to accept this insult.

Boadicea gathered together the warriors of her tribe and led them to the Roman city of Colchester. There she massacred every Roman to be found and burnt the city to the ground. She then marched on London and destroyed that city, too. Builders digging foundations in the city recently found the severed heads of the Romans Boadicea killed during her sacking of the city.

Meanwhile the frantic Roman Governor, Suetonius Paulinus, was hurrying his troops to meet the wild, Celtic host. One force was caught in an ambush and wiped out but a second army gathered north-west of London. This army, led by Suetonius himself, took up a defensive position and awaited the attack of Boadicea. The disciplined Romans easily defeated Boadicea's tribal host and slew some eighty thousand of the Iceni. Boadicea killed herself rather than be taken prisoner. The kingdom of the Iceni became part of the Roman province of Britain.

Tamerlane

The Asian ruler, Tamerlane, was one of the greatest conquerors of history. He led his powerful warriors on campaigns covering thousands of kilometres and defeated his foes.

Tamerlane made himself Emir of Turkestan in 1369 by murdering his brother-in-law. He then built up a formidable army of fierce, mounted tribesmen and welded them into a superbly disciplined, fighting force. In 1381 he captured the wealthy land of Khorassan before moving on to conquer Afghanistan and Persia.

Each of these countries was then ruthlessly plundered of anything of value so that Tamerlane could pay his ferocious warriors. As his fame grew, more and more men flocked to join his army and gain a share of the plunder. Soon his army was the largest in Asia but he still favoured well disciplined horsemen.

In 1393 he conquered Syria and Armenia. Then he turned his horsemen north and overran much of eastern Russia, reaching as far as Moscow before turning back. India was his next target with Delhi being looted and destroyed.

When the city of Isphahan rebelled, Tamerlane was furious. He stormed into the city and killed all the adult men. A huge mound of seventy thousand heads was built near the city to warn others not to rebel.

In 1404 Tamerlane gathered his largest-ever army and set off to invade China but he died on the way. Without their brilliant leader, the troops turned back from the Chinese campaign and the army disbanded. His mighty empire had been built on plunder and loot. It collapsed soon after his death.

Abraham Lincoln

Abraham Lincoln was the most famous President of the United States of America. He was President when the War between the Northern and Southern States broke out and it was his leadership which led the North to victory.

Lincoln was born in a log cabin in the backwoods in the State of Kentucky in 1809. He worked on boats and in a store for several years but in 1837 he qualified as a lawyer and became more prosperous.

Elected to the American Congress in 1847, Lincoln led a low-key career until 1854 when he made a famous speech against slavery. In 1860 he was elected President. Almost at once the Southern States, where slavery was supported, broke away from the Union.

Lincoln decided that the Union of States must be held together and ordered the army to force the Southern States to rejoin the Union.

This led to the Civil War which raged until 1865 and cost hundreds of thousands of lives.

After victory was gained, Abraham Lincoln set himself the task of pulling the nation together again. However, while at the theatre on April 14th 1865, Lincoln was murdered by John Wilkes Booth, a well-known actor.

Chapter Three
MYTHS AND LEGENDS

In countries all over the world myths and legends abound. Some are based on people who really lived such as Dick Turpin, the highwayman, Canute, the Danish king of England, and Dick Whittington.

Many others are based on age-old tales whose origins have been lost in the mists of time. They tell of superhuman heroes like Odysseus, the king of Ithaca, Jason, the Greek, and supernatural creatures like the Trolls from Scandinavia.

They all add up to a veritable world of wonder.

Dick Whittington

Sir Richard Whittington actually lived six hundred years ago. He became a very successful merchant who was Lord Mayor of London four times but in legend he is a poor boy who runs away to seek his fortune.

On Highgate Hill just outside London he stops to rest. There he hears the distant bells of London and they seem to say to him, "Return, Dick Whittington, Lord Mayor of London." Dick returns and with the aid of his faithful cat he has many adventures.

At last he does become Lord Mayor.

Hiawatha

The Indian hero, Hiawatha, was a member of the Iroquois tribe who lived in the eastern forests of the United States of America.

Hiawatha was a great hunter who was a better shot with a bow and arrow than any other man. He also had a pair of magical gloves, which gave him great strength, and magical moccasins, which allowed him to run very quickly. According to early tales, Hiawatha was sent by the Great Spirit to persuade the many tribes to live in peace with each other and to concentrate on agriculture instead of on war.

In 1855 the story of Hiawatha was used by the famous poet, Henry Wadsworth Longfellow, as the basis for an epic poem. Longfellow added other native stories into his long poem. In the poem, Hiawatha marries Minnehaha, daughter of the leader of the Dacotah tribe. Longfellow wove the various tales together to create a great work of fiction. The poem was set to music and became immensely popular.

Blondel

The minstrel, Blondel de Nesle, was a famous musician and poet who became the subject of stories and legends himself.

Blondel was born in Picardy in northern France about 1150. He settled in England and was employed by King Richard the Lionheart. Richard loved music and soon the two men became friends and composed songs together.

In 1190 Richard went on a crusade but, when returning, he was captured by the Duke of Austria. Nobody knew where Richard was being held prisoner. Blondel decided to find out. He travelled around Austria for many months. Outside each castle Blondel would sing a special love song that he and Richard had written and which nobody else knew.

Finally, after much searching, Blondel came to Durrenstein. When he sang his song there he heard a voice joining in the chorus and knew that Richard was held prisoner there. Blondel hurried back to England and arranged for the negotiations which led to Richard's release.

King Arthur

Arthur is the greatest hero of Britain. Dozens of exciting stories are told about him and his knights.

According to the legends, Arthur was the son of King Uther but was brought up by a simple knight after Uther was killed. One day a magical block of stone with a sword embedded in it was found. The wizard, Merlin, explained that only the true King of Britain could pull the sword from the stone. All the bravest knights and lords tried but all failed. Later, Arthur pulled the sword by mistake and revealed himself to be the true King. Arthur was given a magical sword, called Excalibur, by the Lady of the Lake.

Arthur then organised all the great lords and knights into a fellowship which sat at a Round Table so that no one knight would be superior to another. The knights of the Round Table undertook many adventures. Sir Gawain, for instance, went in search of a mysterious, green knight who could have his head chopped off and yet still live. Sir

Gereint undertook many adventures when looking for a wife. Sir Percival fought the Witch of the Waste City while searching for the beautiful Blanchefleur.

The greatest quest of all was the search for the Holy Grail, the cup used by Christ at the Last Supper. During this quest many knights died or became lost. Eventually, a civil war broke out when Arthur's nephew, Mordred, led a rebellion. In the great battle at Camlann, Mordred was killed and Arthur was so badly wounded that a magical barge took him to the land of Avalon far away in the western ocean. His magical sword was thrown into a lake where it was caught by the Lady of the Lake.

The most complete version of these stories was written by a poet, named Sir Thomas Malory, in about 1469 but other versions and other stories exist.

The legendary King Arthur is probably based on a real man who lived about the year AD 500. He led the British fight against the invasions of the Saxons and Angles after the Roman Empire collapsed. About AD 520, Arthur won a great victory at the Battle of Badon Hill. For many years afterwards the Saxons launched no new invasions. Some years later Arthur was killed at Camlann. Little else is known about the real Arthur, except that he was a hero who inspired the later legends.

The Trolls

In the Norse legends Thor is the God of Thunder. Sif is his wife. When Thor learned that Red Loki, the mischievous Fire God, had cut off his wife's hair while she was sleeping, Thor was furious. He seized Red Loki and ordered him to restore Sif's hair. "Or I'll break every bone in your body," Thor threatened.

In fear, Red Loki rushed to the Trolls who were dwarfs living underground. They were so clever they were able to make anything.

Red Loki rashly bet his head that the Trolls would be unable to help him. He thought they would do their best to make new hair for Thor's wife if in exchange they could have his head, for the Trolls feared Red Loki. The Trolls made new hair of real gold that would grow on Sif's head. Red Loki fled in case the Trolls cut off his head. Thor was so pleased he told them they must not cut off Red Loki's head. Instead the Trolls sewed up his lips so that Red Loki could never speak again.

William Tell

Once again the land of Switzerland was fighting a war of independence against an invader. This time it was power-hungry Austria. The invasion took place over six hundred years ago. The Austrians treated the Swiss people cruelly.

One of the bravest Swiss warriors was a man named William Tell, a well-known master archer.

One day, an Austrian, named Gessler, put his hat on a high pole and gave orders that every person passing the pole should bow obediently, so admitting that Gessler was their overlord. Gessler was a sheriff's officer.

It happened that William Tell lived in the part of the country where Gessler ruled. Fearlessly, he refused to lower his head to Gessler's hat. In fury, Gessler ordered him to shoot an apple from the head of his son. Gessler knew there was every chance that Tell would kill the boy if he missed.

William managed to shoot the apple off his son's head and then killed Gessler with his next arrow.

King Midas

One of the famous, Greek legends is that of King Midas, the King of Phrygia. He was extremely mean and greedy. One day he invited Silenus, a demi-god, to come and join in a royal feast. Midas knew that Silenus loved eating and drinking. After he had eaten his fill, Silenus told Midas he would grant him any wish he cared to make.

"I wish that everything I touch will turn to gold," Midas said. Silenus granted Midas his wish and departed. Left alone, King Midas picked up a china goblet. At once it turned to gold. So did everything else that Midas touched, including every piece of food he tried to eat. When he touched his daughter, she, too, turned to gold. Midas was desolate and begged Silenus to remove the golden touch.

"Wash your hands in the magical waters of the River Pactolus," grinned Silenus. Midas did so and the golden touch was taken from him forever.

Robin Hood

From 1189 to 1199, England was ruled by the brave king Richard I, known throughout Europe as "the Lionheart".

One day, he was captured by his enemy, Leopold, Duke of Austria, and locked up in a faraway castle. He would be freed only when a very heavy ransom was paid. While he was away, his crafty brother, Prince John, governed the country with great cruelty.

Many gallant knights refused to pay John's brutal taxes. Among these was Robert, Earl of Huntingdon. Instead of fleeing the country, as did so many other nobles, Robert chose to stay and fight Prince John.

He set up a secret camp in Sherwood Forest and led a band of daring outlaws. The Earl of Huntingdon became known as Robin Hood and did many brave deeds.

He and his Merry Men were still fighting when King Richard at last returned to England and put an end to Prince John's wicked rule.

Dick Turpin's Ride to York

The story of Dick Turpin's ride has been featured in many films shown in cinemas and on television. It is, of course, fiction.

Turpin is often depicted as an heroic highwayman who has been unjustly outlawed. In fact, though, he was a butcher's apprentice who had to flee for dear life when he was revealed as a cattle-stealer.

On the run, he joined a gang of ruthless burglars and later turned to highway robbery when the gang was broken up by officers of the law. One night, he was riding along the road from London to Cambridge when he saw a well-dressed man riding towards him. At once Turpin called on the man to, "Stand and deliver!" but the man just burst out laughing. He, too, was a well-known highwayman, by name Tom King.

"Come, Master Turpin," he cried. "I know you even if you don't know me. Perhaps, though, you have heard of me."

The two men became firm friends but later Dick was to kill Tom accidentally when they were ambushed by police constables. Tom was seized so Dick aimed at one of his captors and fired. The bullet killed Tom.

It is at this point in the famous book, "Rookwood", written by Harrison Ainsworth, that Dick mounts his horse, Black Bess, and, in a sudden fit of bravado, commences his great ride to York. He rides Bess all the way until, as York is reached, Bess drops dead.

It was this book that first launched the legend of Dick Turpin's 'Ride to York'.

The ride may well be untrue but it is a fact that it was in York that Dick Turpin was finally arrested, charged with horse-stealing and hanged.

King Canute

Canute, the most famous Danish king of England, was always being flattered and praised unduly by the people who thronged his court. True, Canute was a proud, powerful and successful ruler who had fought his way to the throne of England but at last he grew tired of being told by his courtiers that he was such a wonderful man who could do anything.

Legend tells us that, one day, Canute ordered his courtiers to follow him to the seashore. His throne was set down on the edge of the lapping waves as the tide came in. Canute stretched out his hand towards the incoming waves and cried, "I command you to stay." Of course, the water continued to come in, whereupon the king rose to his wet feet and spoke to the onlookers behind him. "Listen to me. I want to hear no more empty words of praise from you. You see how worthless is the power of kings."

The courtiers who sought power and rich rewards by over-praising their great king had learned a lesson they would not soon forget.

George and the Dragon

St George is the patron saint of England and one of the most famous saints in Christianity. However, nobody is certain how much of the story about him is true.

According to the legend, George was born in Cappadocia in the late third century. He was a soldier but abandoned his career when he became a Christian.

While travelling through the eastern Mediterranean he came to a city which was plagued by a dragon. Each week the dragon demanded a beautiful girl. The day George arrived it was the turn of the king's daughter to die. George at once set out to slay the dragon and rescue the girl. After a terrific fight he killed the dragon and carried its head into the city.

After several other adventures, George was captured by the pagan Emperor Diocletian and executed on 23rd April 303 in Lydda, Palestine. St George is usually shown on horseback, armed with a lance and killing the dragon. His symbol is a red cross on a white field.

Many people believe that the tale of the dragon is a confused version of George destroying a pagan religion which involved human sacrifice.

Jason and the Golden Fleece

The story of Jason comes from Ancient Greece. It was a popular story told by travelling poets.

According to the legend, Jason was the son of the king of Iolcus. When the king was murdered by a relative named Pelias, Jason, who was a baby, was taken into hiding by loyal servants.

Pelias was warned by an oracle to beware of a 'man with one sandal'. Years later Jason returned to Iolcus and lost a sandal when swimming a river. Pelias was attending a religious ceremony when he saw Jason standing nearby. He was terrified of the young man and decided to send him on a dangerous mission. Pelias promised Jason that he could become king if he brought the Golden Fleece to Iolcus. The Golden Fleece was kept by the king of Colchis. It had magical properties and gave its owner great wealth.

Jason accepted the challenge. He drew together a group of heroes to sail with him in his ship, the Argos. The heroes were known as the Argonauts after their ship. They included Orpheus, the world's most beautiful singer, and Heracles, the strongest man on earth.

The Argonauts encountered many adventures on the way to Colchis. In Colchis, King Aetes promised Jason the Golden Fleece if he would first slay a monster and sow its teeth in a field he had ploughed with two fire-breathing bulls. Aetes had a daughter named Medea who fell in love with Jason. She gave him a magical potion which enabled him to carry out this task.

Aetes tried to trick Jason by not telling him a snake guarded the Golden Fleece but Jason managed to escape the snake and carry the Golden Fleece away with him. Medea went with Jason in the Argos.

After even more adventures, Jason arrived in Iolcus and took the kingdom from Pelias.

The Trojan Horse

No one is quite sure how much of this story is myth and how much history. According to the ancient writer, Homer, it took place about 1194 BC. Paris, son of Priam, King of Troy, kidnapped Helen, the beautiful wife of Menelaus, King of Sparta. Menelaus set out with an army of Greeks in a mighty fleet to rescue her. Helen's lovely face has become famous as "the face that launched a thousand ships".

Troy was a walled city and its siege lasted ten years. Then the Greek, Odysseus, ordered a huge, wooden horse to be built and hid inside it with eleven other warriors. The remaining Greek army then sailed away, as if tired of the war. The Trojans were overjoyed and came out from their city delighted with their new freedom. They saw the wooden horse and dragged it into their city. After dark, Odysseus and his Greeks crept out of the horse, a signal was sent to the Greek fleet to return and Troy was captured. Helen returned to Sparta with Menelaus and as the present of the Trojan horse had proved so fatal the saying "Beware of Greeks bearing gifts" was coined.

Brave Gelert

Gelert was a legendary hound belonging to Llewellyn, a famous, fighting prince of Wales.

One day, on returning home, Llewellyn found Gelert crawling to meet him, covered with blood. Going into his home, the prince found the signs of a struggle and the cradle of his only son overturned and much spattered with blood. Assuming that Gelert had killed and eaten the baby, Llewellyn, in a towering fury, drew his sword and slew the dog.

However, within minutes Llewellyn found his son alive and nearby the body of a huge wolf. Gelert had fought and killed the wolf in defence of the little boy. Too late, Llewellyn was filled with bitter remorse. He buried the hound at Beddgelert in Wales where for many years the grave was pointed out to passing travellers. Beddgelert is in the Welsh county of Gwynedd.

Similar stories of brave dogs are found in Persian and Arabian legends.

The King and the Beggar Maid

It is said that long ago there lived a rich king named Cophetua.

This king was unmarried, much to the annoyance of his subjects who wanted their king to have a son and heir. However, King Cophetua was difficult to please. Beautiful, clever and even quite rich princesses came visiting, hoping that he would propose marriage but King Cophetua never did.

Then, one day, the king looked out of his castle window at a group of beggars. Amongst them was the loveliest maiden he had ever seen. He went out and threw a purse of gold coins amongst the beggars who scrambled for them at once - all except the lovely maiden. The gold meant nothing to her. She was entranced by the king and stared at him with the same love in her eyes that he felt for her. They were married and lived happily ever after. King Cophetua had found a wife at last.

Pegasus

Life was difficult for young heroes in the mythical days of ancient Greece. They had human enemies and fierce monsters to combat.

Handsome, young Bellerophon wished to marry Philonoe, the daughter of King Iobates of Lycia. Nothing should have been more straightforward. Bellerophon went to see Iobates, taking with him, as he thought, a letter of recommendation from King Proteus, his so-called friend. However, far from saying what a hero Bellerophon was, Proteus's letter asked King Iobates to kill him. Not wishing to be blamed for doing this, Iobates set Bellerophon the task of killing the Chimaera, a monster with the head of a lion and the body of a goat. Iobates thought the Chimaera would kill Bellerophon, and he, Iobates, would not be blamed.

Luckily for Bellerophon, the goddess Athene was on his side. She told him where to find a winged horse called Pegasus which would help him slay the Chimaera. Flying on the back of this magical creature, Bellerophon slew the Chimaera, overcame all his enemies and finally married the lovely Philonoe. Then Pegasus flew up into the sky where he was made into a constellation of stars.

46

Beowulf

Beowulf was an Anglo-Saxon hero said to have lived in the ninth or tenth century. At that time a terrible fiend named Grendel was killing the warriors of King Hrothgar of Denmark. No locked door could keep him out. Swords did not harm him, but night after night he would silently slay thirty warriors at a time leaving nothing but bloodstains for their companions to find in the morning.

The fearless Beowulf went to Hrothgar's great hall. He sat up waiting until Grendel walked in with his red eyes glowing. Beowulf seized Grendel with his bare hands and would not let go. Grendel escaped only by wrenching his body away from his arm. Then he bled to death on the way back to his lair. All was not over yet. Beowulf had to destroy Grendel's even more fearsome mother. This he did and the land was safe.

The Flying Dutchman

Long ago a fearless, Dutch captain was sailing off the coast of Africa when a mighty storm blew up. His crew begged him to put into shelter but he laughed and cursed and vowed he would get to the Cape of Good Hope without stopping even if it meant he would have to keep on sailing for ever.

Unfortunately, Satan was listening to his boastful talk. He put a curse on the captain and condemned him to sail the seas for ever. Once every seven years he would be permitted to go ashore and if he could find a young woman willing to marry him the curse would be lifted. Year after year the captain sailed the seas, with his desperate crew growing more haggard-looking and the ship more strained and ragged. No one married him. The curse was never lifted. Sailors say the Flying Dutchman is sailing still.

The Pied Piper

The Pied Piper was a mysterious fellow dressed in clothes of many colours. He visited the town of Hamelin in Germany many years ago.

In those far off days a plague of huge, black rats was tormenting the town. Nothing the townsfolk could do would get rid of them.

The weird piper said he would rid the town of rats for a shilling a head. The town councillors swiftly agreed. The piper played a tune on his pipe and all the rats followed him out of town and were drowned in the river. However, the town council gave the piper far less money than had been agreed.

The piper was angry and played a strange tune on his pipe. This time it was the children of the town who followed him. They danced out of town and into a cave in the mountain which closed after them. They were never seen again. A lame boy, who had not been able to keep up with the other children, came back to tell the story.

Some people believe this legend is a muddled version of the true story of the time when children were persuaded to go on the Children's Crusade. Almost none of them came back.

Some people think it commemorates the Black Death, a plague when thousands of people died of an illness spread by rats.

Chapter Four
DANGEROUS JOURNEYS

On foot, on horseback, in mule- and ox-drawn wagons, on snow-shoes and sledges, in ships and on rafts, by aircraft and in automobiles, men and women have journeyed the countries of the world, from north to south, from east to west.

Explorers and pioneers, warriors and aviators, they have all answered the mysterious call that takes a person from the safety of home to trackless wastes, across tempestuous seas, suffering hardships and starvation and death. Their adventures are summed up in one word - heroism.

The Oregon Trail

In 1843 the United States government offered six hundred and forty acres of land in the far-western territory, known as Oregon, to any man who could successsfully make the journey. One hundred and sixty acres were offered to every wife and to every child.

That year two hundred families gathered in the town of Independence, Missouri, and set off in their wagons. Many died during the two-thousand-mile crossing of mountains, rivers and deserts. This epic journey has made the Oregon Trail world-famous.

Westward with Columbus

In 1492 nobody in Europe knew what lay beyond the western coast of Ireland. Some scholars thought that the world was probably round but not everyone believed them. Even the scholars did not agree on how large the world was.

Then an Italian sailor came up with a startling, new theory and set out to prove that it was true. His discoveries changed the way people thought about the world and the lands on it. His name was Christopher Columbus and he discovered America.

Columbus was born in Genoa in about 1450 to a prosperous, weaving family. After attending some lectures at Pavia University, Columbus joined the family business. In about 1466, however, he went to sea and had many adventures. He quickly learnt the skills of navigation and became famous for his ability to guide a ship to distant lands. In 1476 he settled in Lisbon with his brother who ran a map-making business. Columbus later married the daughter of a wealthy, Portuguese merchant and travelled to the Canary Islands to look after his business.

It was during these years that Columbus

On August 3rd Columbus set sail with a fleet of three ships. The largest was Columbus's own and was named the "Santa Maria". It was only thirty metres long.

For many days the fleet sailed westward, covering thousands of kilometres but, on October 10th the crews demanded that they turn around and return home. They were worried that the ships did not have enough food and water for the long voyage back to Spain and feared that Columbus was leading them into dangerous waters. Columbus was certain they were near China, but promised to turn back if no land was sighted within three days. Two days later the fleet came within sight of an island surrounded by white cliffs which shone in the starlight.

Columbus thought he had reached islands off the east coast of China. In fact he was in the Bahamas. Columbus visited several islands, collecting things such as parrots and tobacco which were new to Europeans. Then he set off to take the good news to Spain. He escaped sinking in a storm and being captured by Portuguese warships to reach Spain on March 15th 1493. The news spread quickly and Columbus later made three more voyages to explore the islands he had discovered. It was not until after his death (in 1506) that people realised that the new lands were not part of China but an entirely new continent which became known as America.

developed his great theory. He read about the travels of Marco Polo and learnt that far to the east of Europe were China and Japan. Both countries were very rich and produced valuable goods such as silk and porcelain. Columbus also believed the theories about the world being round. He reasoned that if he could sail far enough to the west he would arrive in China by a much safer route than travelling overland through Persia and Mongolia. The question was, how far to the west was China?

Columbus undertook many calculations and decided China was five thousand kilometres west of Portugal. In fact it is eighteen thousand kilometres. However, Columbus believed a voyage of five thousand kilometres could be made safely. He needed money though, to pay for ships and sailors.

In 1484, Columbus took his plans to King John II of Portugal, but was turned down. Columbus then approached the King and Queen of Spain. However, Spain was engaged in a war to drive the Moors out of the Spanish province of Granada. Columbus was told to wait. Eventually, in 1492, the Spanish monarchs agreed to pay for Columbus's expedition.

Burke and Wills

For many years after Europeans settled on the coast of Australia nobody knew what lay in the centre of the vast continent.

In 1860 Robert Burke, an Irish explorer, and a surveyor, William Wills, planned to cross the great continent from south to north and back again. In August Burke left Melbourne with a large expedition which was fully equipped for the long journey. Burke brought twenty-five camels from India. He also bought large supplies of food and medicines as well as many scientific instruments to map and measure the interior and collect plant specimens.

All went well until the party reached Menindee. Here some of them quarrelled with Burke and went home. Burke and Wills pushed on to Cooper's Creek. Burke became impatient waiting for supplies and on December 16th he decided to push on north without them. With him went Wills, Charles Gray and John King. He left William Brahe at Cooper's Creek to await supplies.

It took Burke eight weeks of hard travelling to reach the north coast and ten weeks to return to Cooper's Creek. But the camp was deserted. Brahe had been forced to return to Melbourne. He had left only hours before Burke and Wills arrived.

It was three months before a rescue party returned. Only King was left alive. He had been befriended by a tribe of Aborigines who gave him shelter and food in return for his shooting birds for them. The bodies of Burke and Wills were taken back to Melbourne and given a magnificent funeral. Although they had died, their notes and maps proved invaluable to later travellers.

With Scott to the South Pole

By 1850 the coast of Antarctica had been explored and mapped but nobody had travelled very far into the interior. Then, in 1901, a British naval officer, Robert Scott, at the age of thirty-three, took command of a large expedition sent to Antarctica by the Royal Geographical Society. He stayed away for nearly two years and returned with a vast mass of scientific data collected by his team.

In 1910 Scott set out again. As before, his expedition was made up of scientists and surveyors. At the last minute Scott heard that the Norwegian, Roald Amundsen, was also heading for the Pole.

Scott spent the first few weeks in Antarctica on scientific research. On November 1st he set out for the Pole. For weeks Scott and his team battled against blizzards and treacherous snowfields. On January 17th 1912 they reached the South Pole. Scott was bitterly disappointed when he saw the Norwegian flag flying. Roald Amundsen had got there first.

The return journey of thirteen hundred kilometres was even worse than that to the Pole. By March 15th one of the team, Captain L. Oates, was desperately ill. In order not to slow down the others, he walked away into a blizzard and died. "It was the act of a brave man," wrote Scott in his journal.

Oates's sacrifice was in vain. Two weeks later the rest of the party was trapped by a blizzard and ran out of food. They were just seventeen kilometres from the next food store and safety. By March 30th they were dead. They were found eight months later together with the scientific data they had collected. Scott's last journey had been an heroic feat of endurance and scientific exploration.

Robert Peary

Robert Peary was the first man to reach the North Pole. Peary was an officer in the American Navy when, in 1891, he led a sledging expedition to explore northern Greenland. Over the following years he led many teams in the frozen north.

In 1908 he led a team which sailed as far north as possible before transferring to dog sledges on the frozen Arctic Ocean. On April 6th 1909, Peary and his men reached the North Pole. He planted the American flag, took a photograph and headed home. Some people thought that Peary had miscalculated and had not really reached the North Pole at all but an inquiry found in Peary's favour.

Charles A Lindbergh

In 1919 two ex-Royal Flying Corps (the fore-runner of the Royal Air Force) airmen, named John Alcock and Arthur Whitten Brown, were the first men to fly non-stop across the Atlantic Ocean.

The brave flight took them sixteen hours twelve minutes from Newfoundland to Ireland, where they landed safely.

Then for nine years, the world waited to see who would be the first, intrepid aviator to fly the Atlantic on his own.

At eight o'clock in the morning of Friday, May 20th 1928, a brave, American airman, named Charles A Lindbergh, took off from Roosevelt Field, New York, in an attempt to fly to France solo. His aircraft had been named "The Spirit of St Louis". Today that name, like that of Lindbergh, stands high in the annals of flying achievement.

Thirty-three hours and five minutes later, Lindbergh landed safely at Le Bourget airfield in Paris. It was the evening of May 21st. He was greeted by a howling, cheering mob and carried round, shoulder high, for the next half-hour. Then he was taken to a hotel for a well-earned sleep before the many celebrations that followed during the days before he returned to his own, proud country.

Hugh Glass

In the year 1823 the American West was mostly unexplored wilderness. A band of fur trappers under the command of Major Andrew Henry was in the region of what is today known as South Dakota.

Fierce, Arikara tribesmen were on the warpath and Major Henry sent out two trappers to scout out the land. One of those trappers was a well-known frontiersman named Hugh Glass.

The two trappers did not meet any Arikaras but they did blunder into a grizzly bear's den. Glass was grabbed and savaged by the huge beast's claws.

Both scouts yelled for help and the rest of the fur trappers sped to their rescue. Hugh Glass was in a terrible state and seemed close to death.

Major Henry was now very nervous about a possible attack by the Arikaras. The Major thought that Glass was dying and promised half a year's wages to any man who would stay with him until he died. Two men volunteered and the rest of the party departed. For six days Hugh Glass lingered close to death.

His two guards grew scared at being left on their own for so long. They feared that the Arikaras might attack and kill them so they took Hugh's weapons, slipped away and rejoined Major Henry's party two days later.

Behind them Hugh Glass recovered his senses. He had been robbed of everything. Even so, half-starved, he set out to crawl back to Fort Kiowa one hundred and forty kilometres away.

Tortured with thirst and lack of food, Hugh took several weeks to reach the fort. He had just one thought - revenge! For he hated the two trappers who had deserted him. After many weeks, Glass dragged himself to the gates of Fort Kiowa.

Willing hands carried him inside and he was gradually nursed back to health. After a search he found one deserter and forgave him. The other man had joined the Army and Hugh Glass did not bother to search for him.

Will Adams

In 1934, the town of Gillingham, in Kent, honoured William Adams with a clock-tower memorial in Watling Street.

Will was born there in 1575, during the reign of the first Queen Elizabeth. He was apprenticed as a sailor when he was only twelve years old. He later became pilot-major in Rotterdam to a large fleet of Dutch sailing ships bound for the Far East.

The ship on which Will sailed was the only one finally to reach Japan on April 19th 1600. All the other ships had been scattered and many lost in the terrifying storms they had encountered. It was a very dangerous journey.

The great Lord Iyeyasu Tokugawa, ruler of Japan, wanted to meet the foreign sailors. Will was chosen to go to Tokugawa's Court.

The ruler liked Will and, although Will and his comrades wanted to return to Holland, they were forced to remain in Japan. Two years passed and the ruler allowed the crew to return home but Will was kept at court where he became Tokugawa's trusted friend. The ruler made him a nobleman of Japan.

Will remained in Japan for the next thirteen years. Had he wanted to, he could then have returned home but instead he joined the East India Company and became second-in-command of an English settlement which was founded in Japan in 1613.

Returning from a voyage to Siam one day, Will learned of the death of Tokugawa and although the new ruler did not like foreigners, Will remained in Japan until he died in 1620. Gillingham, though, has never forgotten him.

Sir Henry Morton Stanley

In 1871 the world was asking, "Where is Doctor David Livingstone?"

He was the famous, Scottish missionary and explorer who had worked hard in Bechuanaland and led several expeditions; discovering the Zambesi River in 1851, the Victoria Falls in 1855 and Lake Nyasa in 1859. The British Government and the Geographical Society gave Livingstone a thousand pounds to return to Africa in 1866 to find the source of the River Nile.

From then on for the next five years nothing more was heard from the doctor.

In the United States at that time a well-known, English journalist named Henry Morton Stanley was working for the New York Herald. The newspaper sent Stanley to Africa to search for Livingstone.

With two British seamen and two hundred natives, Stanley set out. Ahead of the expedition lay more than thirteen hundred and fifty kilometres. Famine and fever, treachery and starvation, attacks from wild beasts, all these Stanley and his band suffered. At long last, though, Stanley met Livingstone who, enduring many miseries himself, had discovered Lake Tanganyika. "Doctor Livingstone, I presume?" was Stanley's famous greeting as the two men met at last. Stanley was later knighted.

Samuel Baker

Somewhere to the west of Lake Victoria (Victoria Nyanaza) in Africa, natives in 1863 were saying there was a lake into which the River Nile flowed. If this were so, then to find the lake would be a very important discovery. A brave explorer, named Samuel Baker, and his wife assembled a party of porters and set out through the jungle heat to find out if there really was a lake.

The explorer and his wife tramped along with their train of donkeys and camels, following the tracks of the slave-trade caravans.

They had not gone very far when a local tribe decided to attack them. They had been mistaken for slave traders. Baker handed rifles to his men and the tribesmen fled.

Ahead, though, lay more similar dangers, this time from a tribe led by a man who called himself King Kamrasi. In spite of Baker and his wife both falling ill at this time, they managed to get clear of Kamrasi and his warriors. At last they were close to their journey's end. Suddenly they came within sight of the lake for which they were searching. Baker named it Lake Albert (Albert Nyanaza) after Queen Victoria's husband.

Marco Polo

Nicolo and Maffeo Polo were two Italian brothers who had just returned in 1270 from a mission to China which had lasted ten years. In those days little, if anything, was known about the Great Kublai Khan, lord of the Tartars, who lived in China.

Nicolo Polo had a son named Marco who was then just seventeen years of age. As he listened to his father and uncle talking about their adventures in China he wished he had been old enough to go with them. Now, though, Nicolo and Maffeo were talking about returning for they had made a lot of money. They knew that if they returned they would be able to make more money. Marco was overjoyed when he realised he would be going with them.

It took the three Polos three years to reach the court of the Great Khan. At last a wayfarer pointed to a noble, white building. "There you will find the Great Khan," said he. Marco's heart must have jumped

excitedly as he urged his horse forward.

Nicolo introduced his son to Kublai Khan who was delighted with the young Venetian.

Marco liked the Tartars and would often go through the streets talking to the farmers and shopkeepers and traders who were proud of the bolts of silk they were selling.

Very soon Marco became a great favourite at court. He was given honours and titles and his advice was eagerly sought.

The three Polos became very well-known, Marco especially. The day came when Kublai Khan made him governor of the city of Chang-yow.

Eventually, the Polos longed to return to Venice. So they asked the Great Khan for a passport. Without one they knew it would be impossible to make a safe journey through the lands of the warlike Tartars where they were not known. However, the Khan refused to give them this necessary passport, for he had become fond of the Polos and relied very much on their advice.

Then in the year 1292, the Shah of Persia asked the Great Khan to send him a wife. For this honour, a princess was chosen from

the Khan's court. The journey to Persia was long and dangerous and none of the Khan's subjects was willing to undertake such a mission. None that is except the three Polos for they knew that once they were in Persia they would be free to return to Venice.

Eventually the Khan agreed that they should escort the princess to Persia.

On the day they left, they stood before the Khan, now dressed in their rough, travelling clothes. "I know I can trust you, Marco," said the Khan, "to see that the princess arrives safely and then to return here." With fourteen ships and nearly two thousand sailors, the three Polos set out with the princess for Persia. The ships at last reached their destination but sad news awaited them. Kublai Khan had died while they were at sea.

As the Khan was dead the Polos returned to Venice. When they arrived they had been twenty-four years away from the city. The treasures they brought home with them from the East made them rich for the rest of their lives.

Thor Heyerdahl

How the brown-skinned people who live in the tiny islands of the South Pacific had come to live in that part of the world had puzzled men of science for many years.

A clever Norwegian, named Thor Heyerdahl, gave the matter a lot of thought and finally concluded that the inhabitants must have drifted to the islands from Peru.

To prove this, he wanted to build a raft of balsa wood like those used by the islanders and, making use of the prevailing winds and currents, sail the raft from Peru to the islands. The British, American and Peruvian governments liked his idea and gave him financial assistance towards the venture.

On April 28th 1947 the frail craft, named after the Inca god Kon-Tiki, set out from Callao in west Peru. An image of Kon-Tiki was painted on the sail. Heyerdahl and five friends were aboard.

There followed three months at sea, braving tropical storms and mountainous waves as well as dangers from hungry sharks and monstrous whales. Heyerdahl and his five gallant friends finally sighted land after having floated more than seven thousand kilometres from Peru. They headed for the Ravoia atoll in the Tuamotu group of islands and after being swept into a lagoon landed safely on July 21st 1947.

Thor Heyerdahl had proved to the world that the voyage could be carried out safely and that his theory, that the original settlers had sailed to the islands, was correct.

Chapter Five
WARS AND WARRIORS

From the earliest days, and certainly from Biblical times, wars have raged for many reasons. There have been big wars and little wars for thousands of years but in every conflict there have been men and women of outstanding bravery.

Heroes and heroines abound in the histories of countries everywhere. The terrible battles they fought are numbered by the thousand. From kings, such as Leonidas of Sparta, to the peasant girl, Joan of Arc, from battles, such as the Heights of Abraham to Pearl Harbour, the names will endure until the end of time.

Prince Rupert

The most dashing leader of cavalry in the English Civil War that broke out in 1642 was Prince Rupert, the German nephew of King Charles I of England.

Rupert fought for King Charles in many battles, leading the Royalist cavalry.

King Charles lost the war but Prince Rupert continued to fight at sea.

When King Charles II was restored to the throne, Rupert returned to England. He later helped to found the Hudson Bay Company. He died in 1682.

The Alamo

In 1836 the people of Texas were fighting against the Mexican government for freedom and democracy. The first battle of the war was fought at the Alamo, a small mission in the town of San Antonio.

The Alamo blocked the path of a large, Mexican army led by General Santa Anna and was defended by just one hundred and seventy-five Texans led by Colonel William Travis. Among the defenders were the famous frontiersman, Davy Crockett, and Jim Bowie who invented the Bowie knife. On February 22nd Santa Anna arrived and began to bombard the Alamo with his cannon. After the Texans refused an offer of surrender, Santa Anna announced that no prisoners would be taken. On March 6th the Mexican finally sent his army to assault the battered mission. Two attacks were beaten back by the Texans, but a third attack burst through the walls. The Texans fought gallantly but, in the end, they were all killed.

The battle had delayed the Mexican army long enough for the Texans to gather a proper army. Santa Anna was defeated and Texas became independent.

The Somme

The Battle of the Somme in 1916 was one of the longest, most bloody and inconclusive in history.

The First World War was fought between Great Britain, France and Russia against Germany and the Austrian Empire. Great Britain and France declared war on Germany on August 4th 1914. For a few weeks battles raged throughout Belgium and into the heart of France.

By Christmas 1914, though, mobile warfare had ceased, trenches had been dug from the Swiss frontier in the south through to the coast of France in the north and the war had become bogged down.

On the Western Front, Germany faced France and Britain in a merciless war that lasted four more years. All three armies were dug into trenches behind barbed wire.

In 1916 the British and French generals decided to try to break the German lines near the Somme River. The plan called for a massive bombardment of artillery, to smash the trenches and disrupt supply lines, and then infantry would attack to punch a hole through the lines.

Unknown to the British, the Germans had dug deep, storage pits safe from artillery shells and had more than one line of trenches.

On June 23rd the artillery bombardment began. It lasted a week. At dawn on July 1st British and French infantry climbed out of their trenches and advanced on a front of twenty-five kilometres. The Germans were waiting with hidden machine guns and targeted artillery. Although this first attack failed, the British continued with further attacks.

On November 18th the generals realised that the German lines on the Somme were too strong to be taken.

The battle had cost four hundred and eighteen thousand British casualties along with one hundred and ninety-five thousand French and six hundred and fifty thousand German. The British and French had advanced only ten kilometres.

Samurai

The Samurai were fierce warriors from Japan who dominated the country for a thousand years until the 1860s.

The earliest Samurai lived about AD 750. They were elite warriors, trained from birth to be fighters. Samurai were highly skilled in the use of the bow and of the long, slightly curved sword which every Samurai carried. The early Samurai were organised in clans, each based on a family. For many years these Samurai clans fought savage wars for control of Japan.

By 1600 the Tokugawa clan had defeated all its rivals and became masters of Japan. The leader of the Tokugawa ruled Japan on behalf of the Emperor, who took little part in everyday life but was regarded as a god on earth. The Samurai of the Tokugawa period used swords and short swords more than bows and developed a code of honour, called bushido.

This tough code of warrior honour was overthrown in 1868 when power was returned to the Emperor. Merchants and others were then given a say in how the country was run. However, bushido remained a force in Japan. Even today, the concepts of honour and prestige are very important.

Robert E. Lee

Robert E. Lee led the forces of the South during the American Civil War and was the greatest general of that war.

Lee was born in Virginia in 1807 and joined the army in 1825. He served bravely in the Mexican War of 1846 and by 1861 was the commanding officer of the First Cavalry.

When the Civil War broke out he was given command of the Northern forces but chose to fight for his native Virginia on the side of the South. In 1862 he was made commander of the Army of Northern Virginia, the main force of the Southern States.

Aided by General 'Stonewall' Jackson he launched an attack on the Northern troops. At Cedar Run on August 9th and Bull Run three weeks later he defeated his enemies and then succeeded in driving them back towards Washington.

Robert Lee's advance was successfully blocked at Antietam Creek on September 17th when he was outnumbered two to one by a contingent of Northern troops. In May 1863, though, Lee won a great victory at Chancellorsville. His fifty-three thousand troops outflanked a Northern army of seventy-five thousand and forced them to retreat with a loss of over eighteen thousand men.

Regrettably, General 'Stonewall' Jackson was killed on the eve of the battle and Lee lost his best general. In June he launched an invasion of the North but was fought to a standstill by General Meade at Gettysburg on July 3rd.

By 1864 it was clear that the Northern forces, now led by General Grant, were able to field more men and weapons than the South. Lee continued to fight bravely and consistently outmanoeuvred his enemies.

However, by April 1865 it was clear his troops could not last much longer. On April 9th, Lee surrendered to Grant at the Appomattox Court House, the two leaders saluting each other. After the war, Lee became President of Washington College and died in 1870.

Pearl Harbour

The attack on Pearl Harbour in Hawaii was one of the most famous in history. It took place without warning and thousands of men were killed.

In 1941 tension between Japan and the United States of America was growing. Japan had invaded large areas of eastern Asia and was threatening important mineral and oil fields. America lodged protests and made it clear that it would not tolerate further Japanese expansion.

The Japanese government decided that if the expansion was to continue, America must be dealt with. They then decided to declare war on America.

Japanese military men knew that America had a powerful navy in the Pacific. They planned to destroy that navy at the very start of the war. It was decided to attack at the precise moment that war was declared in the hope of surprising the American navy. The main American naval base was at Pearl Harbour in Hawaii. The attack was timed for 8 am on December 7th 1941.

A huge, Japanese fleet set sail for Hawaii and, under the instructions of Admiral Yamamoto (inset), launched an attack with submarines and aircraft.

Surprise was total. Before the Americans could defend their base the Japanese had sunk four battleships and eleven other warships and crippled many others. They had also destroyed two hundred and forty-seven aircraft and killed over two thousand men. Only twenty-nine Japanese aircraft were lost. The Americans were particularly angry because the written declaration of war did not arrive until after the attack began. As a result America was brought into the Second World War.

Balaclava

In 1854 France and Britain were at war with Russia to protect Turkey, which the Russians had attacked. A force of British and French troops landed in the Crimea to capture and destroy Russian bases. On October 25th a large, Russian army advanced against the port of Balaclava, which was being used by the British. Lord Raglan led a British force to block their path.

A massive, Russian, cavalry attack was stopped by the 93rd Highland Regiment and a second smashed by the British Heavy Cavalry Brigade. However, a third Russian force captured a fort and began removing its cannon. The British Light Cavalry Brigade was ordered to stop them. Unfortunately the Light Brigade commander, Lord Cardigan, received a garbled version of the order and led his men towards the wrong guns. To the amazement of those watching, not least the Russians, the Light Brigade poured down the valley, plunged into the Russian positions and sent the enemy fleeing. Exhausted and without support, the Light Brigade then retreated. Out of six hundred and seventy-three men, two hundred and seventy-two were killed and, of the rest, only one hundred and ninety-five were fit for action.

The charge is famous for its heroism.

Battle of Towton

In England in the year 1461 there were two Kings. The elder was King Henry VI who had been defeated in battle by the second king, Edward IV, who was only twenty years of age.

King Henry was a weak man but he had a very strong-minded queen.

Her name was Margaret. She and King Edward both had big armies and were ready to fight a great battle to see who should rule England.

The battle that followed was not the first battle that had taken place between the two sides. The last victor had been Edward. He was in London celebrating his victory and recent coronation.

Queen Margaret, with her husband, King Henry, was in York in the north of England. She was in command of a large army consisting of sixty thousand hard-fighting soldiers.

King Edward gathered an army of forty thousand and marched north. The two forces met on March 29th near the village of Towton, about sixteen kilometres south of York. The battle started at nine o'clock in the morning amid a furious snowstorm.

King Edward's soldiers had the wind directly behind them as they advanced and the blinding snow was blowing straight into the faces of their enemies.

King Edward had given an order that no mercy should be shown if his army won the battle. The desperate struggle went on for five hours. It resulted in complete victory for King Edward. His order to show no mercy was carried out ruthlessly.

The slaughter was terrible. At the time it was reported that no less than thirty thousand soldiers had been slain.

Rorke's Drift

The defence of Rorke's Drift in 1879 was one of the world's most heroic actions, and was later made the subject of an exciting film.

In January of that year a British army invaded the Zulu Empire in South Africa. For many years there had been cattle raids and border disputes between the Zulus and British settlers. The British Lord Chelmsford decided to end the disputes by conquering the Zulu empire.

On January 22nd 1879 the main British force, of over a thousand men, was attacked by the Zulus on the slopes of the mountain Isandhlwana. Nearly all the British were killed - only a few of them escaping.

The British had left a small party of one hundred men to guard the sick and wounded at Rorke's Drift, a ford on the Tugela River. In the late afternoon after the massacre on Isandhlwana four thousand Zulus attacked.

Most of the Zulus had only spears, but some had rifles and all fought with great courage. The British had rifles, but were hampered by the darkness and the overwhelming numbers of the Zulus. All through the night the battle raged. Soon after dawn the Zulus retreated. About four hundred Zulus and twenty-five British had died. Eleven Victoria Crosses and nine Distinguished Conduct Medals for valour were awarded to British soldiers for their heroic defence.

Iwo Jima

Iwo Jima is an island in the Pacific Ocean where a desperate battle was fought in 1945.

The island was of vital, military importance as aircraft based there could be used to bomb Tokyo, the Japanese capital. American generals were determined to capture the island; the Japanese were desperate to stop them.

For months in 1944 the Japanese built complex defences. Underground shelters were constructed to protect troops from bombs and gunfire while long tunnels led to gun positions which could be used to sweep the island and to protect each other. Over twenty-one thousand Japanese troops were placed on the island as an American attack seemed increasingly likely.

On February 16th 1945 the American invasion fleet arrived.

It consisted of seventy thousand Marines supported by battleships, cruisers, aircraft carriers and over eight hundred other ships.

For two days the ships pounded the island with gunfire while aircraft bombed the Japanese positions. At dawn on February 19th the Marines stormed ashore from landing craft. However, many landing craft either sank or were wrecked and the troops became confused. Japanese gunfire inflicted heavy casualties. Eventually the American troops gained a foothold and were able to bring heavy artillery ashore to support the infantry attacks.

However, even then the Japanese did not surrender for they had orders to defend the island to the death. The Americans had to bring in reinforcements on February 27th. The fierce fighting continued until March 16th. About twenty thousand Americans became casualties while nearly every Japanese soldier was killed.

Joan of Arc

Joan of Arc led a French army against the invading English and managed to restore independence to her nation, although she lost her life in the process.

Joan was born into a simple, farming family in Domremy in 1412. In 1428 she said she had received messages from God in the form of voices and visions of the Saints Catherine and Margaret. The visions told her to save her nation by fighting the English. Joan told her local lord about this, but he thought she was merely a silly girl and sent her home.

In 1429 Domremy itself was sacked by a Burgundian force allied to the English. Joan again heard her voices. A young lord, named Jean de Metz, lent her some men's clothes and arranged for her to meet the Dauphin, heir to the French throne. The Dauphin asked churchmen to question Joan about her visions. When the churchmen declared that Joan was indeed receiving heavenly messages, the Dauphin gave her armour and put her in charge of some troops.

Joan quickly proved herself to be heroically brave in battle and to have a gift for leadership and inspiring her troops. She became a favourite leader of the French soldiers, who believed she had supernatural powers conferred by God. When Joan arrived at Orleans she led a successful attack on the English army. She then moved to Reims and arranged for the Dauphin to be crowned King of France in the cathedral.

Early in 1430 Joan was captured while leading an heroic defence of Compiegne. A new group of churchmen had gathered and they declared that Joan's visions came from the Devil, not from God. On May 30th 1431 she was burnt at the stake for being in league with the Devil.

After her death many miracles were attributed to Joan. In 1919 the Catholic Church recognised her purity of motive and religious feeling by making her a saint.

Leonidas

The Greek king, Leonidas, became famous for his heroic actions at the Battle of Thermopylae in 480 BC.

In that year a vast army of hundreds of thousands of Persians, led by Xerxes, was invading Greece.

The route of the invaders led through the narrow pass of Thermopylae. Leonidas, King of Sparta, led a small army of about three hundred men to block the pass. He hoped to delay the Persians long enough for Greek forces to organise properly. For three days the hopelessly outnumbered Greeks held out, until the Persians found a way through the mountains to attack Leonidas from the rear. Leonidas and all his Spartans were killed in the battle.

The Last Fight of the "Revenge"

In the 1580s and 1590s England and Spain were at war. England had converted to the new Protestant form of Christianity while Spain remained loyal to the Roman Catholic faith. Philip II of Spain was determined to defeat Protestants everywhere. English troops helped the Dutch Protestant rebels while English sailors raided Spanish colonies and ships in the Americas. In 1588 Philip sent his great invasion fleet, the Armada, against England but it was defeated.

Sir Richard Grenville was one of the most famous English sailors who fought against the Spanish. He raided the Americas and fought several battles. In 1591 he and Sir Thomas Howard led some English ships to the Azores to try to capture a Spanish treasure fleet.

However, the Spanish learnt of the plan and sent fifty-three warships to attack the English. Sir Thomas Howard escaped, but Sir Richard Grenville on board the "Revenge" was outmanoeuvred by the Spanish. The Spanish fleet bore down on the lone, English ship and a furious fight broke out. At times the Spanish managed to board the "Revenge", but each time the English drove them back. Cannon from the "Revenge" pounded the Spanish and sank more than one ship. After fifteen hours of fighting only twenty of the crew of the "Revenge" were left alive and the Spanish captured the ship. Sir Richard Grenville was so badly injured that he died a few hours later. The "Revenge" was badly damaged and sank shortly afterwards. The fight became famous throughout Europe and Alfred, Lord Tennyson later wrote the well-known poem about it.

The Heights of Abraham

General James Wolfe was born at Westerham in Kent, England, on January 2nd 1727. He became an officer in his father's Corps of Marines in 1741 and was later transferred to the 12th Regiment of Foot. From then on until 1758 he fought in Europe. He was at the Battle of Culloden when Prince Charles Edward, the Young Pretender known as Bonnie Prince Charlie, and his Scottish Highlanders were defeated by the Duke of Cumberland and his army.

In 1759 Wolfe was chosen to capture the city of Quebec in Canada. From this city France controlled the entire area of Canada.

At this time a great war known as the Seven Years' War was raging. Europe was aflame with war and now the slaughter had spread to North America. In command of the French forces in Canada was the splendid general, the Marquis of Montcalm.

In September 1759 he was in possession of Quebec with a powerful force. The city was on a high point of land, known as the Heights of Abraham, overlooking the St Lawrence River. If Quebec was to be taken by the British they would have to climb the Heights.

To climb in daylight meant the British soldiers could easily be shot before they reached the top. Wolfe knew that they would have to climb at night. He also knew that most of Montcalm's men were guarding the eastern side of the Heights. On September 6th therefore, Wolfe moved his three thousand six hundred men in small boats to the western side. Then, six nights later, Wolfe and a few hundred of his soldiers, under cover of darkness, climbed the Heights and prepared for battle.

When Montcalm learned that the British had climbed the cliff face, he moved swiftly. In the battle that followed both Wolfe and Montcalm were killed. Quebec now belonged to the British who, with it, gained control of Canada.

The Battle of Stalingrad

In June 1941 the most powerful force the world had ever seen was launched by the German High Command against Russia. A terrible war followed. In 1942 the Germans, commanded by General F. von Paulus, struck at Stalingrad, an industrial city which stands on the River Volga. At first it seemed certain that the Germans would capture the city.

Russian soldiers stood at bay in the streets of the battered city, their backs to the river. As the bitter, hand-to-hand fighting went on, the Russian commander-in-chief, General Zhukov, prepared to strike back. He gathered together a huge army and advanced on Stalingrad. The Germans laying siege to the city were encircled and eventually compelled to surrender. It was a terrible defeat for the Germans.

The Battle of Gettysburg

In 1863 the terrible Civil War between the Southern and Northern States of the United States had been raging for nearly three years.

In the middle of June, General Robert E Lee, commanding a Southern army (called Confederates) of seventy-five thousand men, struck northwards in an attempt to advance through Pennsylvania and capture Washington, the capital of the Union. At the same time a huge Northern army (called Unionists) advanced to meet them. The two armies came face to face on July lst at Gettysburg, Pennsylvania.

For three days General Lee delivered one attack after another. It was on the third day of the battle that Lee ordered General George Pickett, who was in command of fifteen thousand picked troops, to charge across an open field against the Unionist centre.

Bravely, Pickett's men raced headlong into a colossal storm of shot and shell. It was more than even those gallant soldiers could stand. Only half of them returned. The Southern army lost the battle.

Lee retreated. The Union had won its first clear-cut victory against the Confederacy. In 1865 the war ended in defeat for the South.

Chapter Six
NAMES TO REMEMBER

Since time began, in all walks of life, thousands of men, women and children have become famous - men such as Thomas Edison, the great inventor, and Neil Armstrong, the first man to step on to the moon, women like Marie Curie, who, with her husband Pierre, first discovered radium, boys like Wolfgang Mozart who could write an opera when he was only twelve years of age. Even would-be assassins, Guy Fawkes for instance, are famous today.

Their stories and many more can be read in the pages that follow.

William Caxton

William Caxton was born about 1422 in Kent, England. He became a wealthy merchant and lived and worked in Bruges, Belgium, for many years. It was there that he learned all that was known about printing at that time. He decided to return to England and set up his own printing press. So it was that William Caxton became the first printer of a book in England. He became so famous that one day King Edward IV, with his wife, visited Caxton and watched his printing press at work.

William Bligh

Captain William Bligh is best known as the captain of HMS "Bounty", a ship of the Royal Navy the crew of which mutinied in the Pacific in 1789. However, Bligh led a long and exciting life quite apart from the famous mutiny.

Bligh was born in 1754 and went to sea as a young man.

He soon became famous as a superb navigator and a fine seaman. Unfortunately, he found it difficult to make friends and was not good at enforcing discipline.

In 1772 he joined Captain Cook on his third voyage to the Pacific. When Cook was killed by a tribe of Hawaiians, it was Bligh who led a small party ashore to rescue his body.

In 1787 William Bligh was selected to command a new expedition to the Pacific. His great skills as a seaman and navigator, combined with the fact that he had sailed in the Pacific before, won him the command.

He set sail in HMS "Bounty" for Tahiti to collect breadfruit plants and take them to the West Indies as a new source of food for the plantations there. Many of the crew enjoyed the life in Tahiti and when Bligh wanted to set sail again some of the men were unhappy. Fletcher Christian, Bligh's Mate, also wanted to stay in Tahiti rather than continue the dangerous voyage with Bligh. However, the "Bounty" did sail.

On April 28th 1789, bound from Tahiti to the Cape of Good Hope, some of the crew, led by Fletcher Christian, mutinied. Bligh and the men loyal to him were put in a small boat and set adrift - over four thousand kilometres from a safe port.

It was Bligh's great skill as a navigator that enabled him to bring his tiny boat to safety in Timor.

Some of the mutineers were later caught and executed, but others hid on Pitcairn Island and were never found.

After the Mutiny on the "Bounty", Bligh continued his career in the navy.

He fought bravely at the Battles of Camperdown and Copenhagen before becoming Governor of New South Wales in 1805.

He died peacefully in 1817.

Grace Darling

On September 7th 1838 the steamship "Forfarshire" ran on to rocks off the Farne Islands in a great storm.

The ship was pounded to pieces and quickly sank but a few survivors managed to swim and crawl on to a rock. The waves swept over the rock and the people were in great danger.

A local girl, called Grace Darling, and her father had seen the wreck and they set out in a small rowing boat to try to save the victims.

Although only a slim girl, Grace steered the boat and pulled at the oars with her father. The pair battled through the waves and rescued several of those who had survived the wreck. Grace Darling was later given a gold medal for her bravery.

Florence Nightingale

The modern profession of nursing was founded by Florence Nightingale, who began training nurses in hygiene and medical matters.

In 1854 Florence learnt that British soldiers wounded during the Crimean War were being housed in very poor conditions at the Turkish town of Scutari. Florence became the leader of a group of thirty-seven nurses and took them to Scutari. Pushing aside the protests of the army command, Miss Nightingale entirely reformed the medical service. The death rate at Scutari fell from 40% to 4%. Every evening, before retiring, she would tour the wards with a lamp to make sure everything was as it should be. The soldiers soon knew her as 'the lady with the lamp' and she was enormously popular.

On her return to England she began training others in her theories of nursing. Before long all hospitals were using her methods. Florence Nightingale died in 1910 after receiving many honours.

Neil Armstrong

Neil Armstrong was the first human ever to walk on the Moon. He made this historic step on July 20th 1969 as part of the Apollo XI mission.

Armstrong was born in 1930. As a young man he flew in the Korean War before becoming a test pilot and later an astronaut.

In 1966 he took part in a dramatic, space adventure on the famous Gemini VIII mission. Armstrong and fellow astronaut David Scott launched on March 16th to spend three days in orbit, carrying out scientific missions. After seven hours the space craft began to twist. Within a few minutes, the Gemini was spinning and tumbling out of control, turning over once every second.

Armstrong realised that a steering rocket was firing continuously, so all the rockets were closed down and the re-entry thrusters were used to stop the spinning. Armstrong and Scott immediately returned to Earth.

The Apollo XI mission went much more smoothly. Together with Buzz Aldrin and Michael Collins, Armstrong took off in a huge Saturn V rocket on July 16th 1969. When the command and lunar module were in orbit the lunar module separated from the command module (which continued to orbit the moon) and descended to the Moon's surface where Armstrong and Aldrin spent some time. They planted an American flag and collected soil samples. Then they returned to the command module and flew back to Earth. They landed safely on July 24th.

Guy Fawkes

Every year, on November 5th, firework parties take place throughout Britain at which an effigy of Guy Fawkes is usually burnt on a bonfire. The reason for this dates back to a treason plot nearly four centuries ago.

In 1605 the new king of England, James I, who was a Protestant, enacted tough laws against the Catholic Church. It was less than twenty years since the Spanish Armada tried to impose Catholicism on England by force and many people believed the Catholic Church wanted to destroy England.

A group of Catholics, led by Robert Catesby, Thomas Percy and Guy Fawkes, decided that the only way that they could worship openly would be to install a Catholic government.

Their plan was to kill the King and his chief supporters by blowing up the House of Lords when the King was present for the Opening of Parliament. The conspirators would then tell all their Catholic friends to rise in rebellion while a foreign army would land to crush the Protestants.

By October 1605 everything was in readiness. Incautiously, one of the Catholic plotters warned his friend, Lord Monteagle, not to attend the Opening of Parliament on November 5th. Lord Monteagle became suspicious and informed the King.

King James realised that there was a plot against him and ordered an investigation. A search was made of the cellars under the House of Lords. There the government soldiers found Guy Fawkes with thirty-six barrels of gunpowder and a fuse.

He was arrested and his fellow plotters were quickly rounded up. After a short trial, Fawkes and his friends were sentenced to death and hung, drawn and quartered.

The people of England were so pleased to have been spared a Catholic rising that they began the tradition of burning a likeness of Guy Fawkes every year on November 5th.

Charles Rolls and Frederick Royce

If a man who can make something that people would like to own meets another man who can sell those products very successfully and they decide that they will set up in business together, then it is quite likely that success will attend their efforts.

So it was with Charles Rolls and Frederick Royce. Royce was a brilliant engineer, born in 1863. He was only twenty-one years old when he formed an engineering firm which he called Royce Limited. He was one of the first men to design and build automobiles.

He made his first car in 1904. Now he needed somebody who could sell his cars. At that time there was another man interested in motor cars. His name was Charles Rolls and he certainly knew how to sell cars successfully.

The two men met and, in 1906, formed a new company called Rolls Royce Limited. The first Rolls Royce car was called Silver Ghost and it was produced for no less than nineteen years.

Today Rolls Royce cars are sold all over the world. Kings and queens, rulers and the richest of the rich are happy to own them. The firm became more successful when aeroplanes came into being and it began to produce engines for the world's airlines.

Thomas Edison

Born in Ohio in 1847, Thomas Edison was one of the world's greatest inventors.

As a boy he only spent a few months at school for his teacher sent him home crying one day. The teacher had told him he was too stupid to learn anything. Edison's mother, once a school teacher, was so angry she refused to send him back to school but taught him herself at home.

He started work as a newspaper boy on a railway, writing and printing his own newspaper. He invented the gramophone in 1877. In 1879 he made the first, practical, electric light-bulb. Later he built a generating station and provided electric lighting for a large part of New York. He made improvements in radio, the telephone and cinematography.

He died in 1931.

The Montgolfier Brothers

Years ago the Chinese celebrated festivals and special events with small balloons made of thin paper and filled with hot air.

In 1783 two brothers, Joseph and Etienne Montgolfier, who lived near Lyon in France, were the first men to make a big balloon that could fly. It was 11.5 metres high and 11.5 metres wide. It was not manned.

The brothers were determined to make a balloon to carry human beings. This they did and, on November 21st 1783, two French aristocrats, named Pilatre de Rozier and the Marquis d'Arlandres, were the first men to make an untethered flight.

Bonnie Prince Charlie

In 1688 the English King, James II, was exiled overseas and the throne was handed jointly to his daughter, Princess Mary, and her husband, Prince William of Orange.

In 1745 James's grandson, Prince Charles Edward Louis Stuart, was determined to regain the throne for himself. He was a tall, handsome, young man, known to history as Bonnie Prince Charlie.

He landed in Scotland on July 25th 1745, determined to gain the throne.

Many Scottish clans gathered round him and, after a victory at Prestonpans, he marched south into England as far as Derby. He was forced to retreat, however, and he and his brave clansmen were defeated at the Battle of Culloden in 1746.

He fled for his life, his one hope of safety being to return to France. He was driven from one hiding place to another. Then he met Flora Macdonald who dressed him as her maid-servant and helped him to escape to France. He died in Italy in 1788.

Sir Francis Drake

One day in 1588, the famous seaman, Sir Francis Drake, was playing bowls at Plymouth with Lord Howard of Effingham, the Lord High Admiral of England. Suddenly, a messenger arrived with news that the Armada, a huge fleet of Spanish vessels, had been sighted in the English Channel. It was an invading force that had been sent by the King of Spain, England's enemy.

Lord Howard wished to abandon the game of bowls. Drake grinned. "Time to finish the game and beat the Spaniards, too," said he.

In the days that followed, the constant harrying of the Spanish by the English ships together with the furious, Channel storms, defeated the Armada.

Drake, born about 1540, was a determined enemy of Spain. He led expeditions to plunder Spanish treasure fleets returning from the Americas. He had destroyed the Spanish fleet in Cadiz harbour in 1587 and had thus 'singed the King of Spain's beard'.

He was the first Englishman to sail round the world and for this Queen Elizabeth knighted him. He died in 1596.

Wolfgang Amadeus Mozart

Mozart, born in 1756, in the Austrian city of Salzburg, was the son of a well-known musician. Amazingly, the young boy started to compose music at the very early age of four. He was only six years old when, with his elder sister Maria Anna (also a first-class musician), he appeared before the Emperor of Austria. They astonished the entire court as they performed on harpsichord and violin.

Their father then took them on a tour that led them to Paris and London where they performed before the royal courts of France and Britain. The Mozarts became famous all over Europe.

Mozart was fourteen years of age when his first opera was played in La Scala Theatre in Milan, Italy. It was an instant success. From then on he wrote more operas, church and chamber-music and became one of the world's greatest composers, dying in 1791.

Michelangelo

Born in Caprese, Italy, in 1475, Michelangelo Buonarroti was taken by his father to Florence when he was a baby. At that time, the city of Florence was the centre of a great movement in art. Artists, sculptors, poets and goldsmiths gathered there, all striving eagerly to produce great works of art.

Michelangelo's father was a magistrate and did not like the idea of his son becoming an artist although the boy showed a wonderful talent when he was only twelve years old. At last his father relented and the boy was apprenticed to a famous painter. It soon became clear that he was a splendid artist.

Soon, though, Michelangelo turned to sculpture. At that time Florence was ruled by the great Duke Lorenzo the Magnificent. Michelangelo came to Lorenzo's notice and, struck by the young man's ability, he took the lad into his own house. It was there that Michelangelo became a great sculptor.

Lorenzo died in 1492 and four years later Michelangelo went to Rome. During the next five years he produced two extraordinary pieces of sculpture. The first was a beautiful figure of the Virgin Mary weeping over the body of her son, Jesus, which today is in the Basilica of St Peter's, Rome. The second was a huge figure of the boy, David, standing ready to fight Goliath. This can be seen in Florence, as splendid as the day Michelangelo finished it.

Michelangelo was also a great painter. In 1512 he completed his great masterpiece. It consisted of one hundred and forty-five pictures painted in the Sistine Chapel in Rome. Most of the work on the ceiling was done with Michelangelo lying on his back.

In 1564 Michelangelo, painter, sculptor, architect and poet, died aged eighty-nine.

Louis Pasteur

In 1877 in France a terrible illness called anthrax was killing many animals. In some districts twenty sheep out of every hundred were dying. The Minister of Agriculture sent for Louis Pasteur, a famous chemist, to find a cure for the disease. Pasteur succeeded. His hard work resulted in a quantity of dead anthrax germs being injected into sheep. Then living anthrax germs were injected. For a few days the sheep were unwell. Then gradually they all recovered.

Once again, Louis Pasteur had succeeded as he had so often with his experiments - he it was who first made milk safe to store by heating and quickly cooling it. Today, it is called pasteurisation after Louis Pasteur.

Amerigo Vespucci

The American continent was discovered by Christopher Columbus but its name came from the explorer, Amerigo Vespucci, who was born in Florence in 1451.

In 1492 Vespucci moved to Seville in Spain to set up business. The lands newly discovered by Columbus interested Vespucci. He made four business-seeking voyages and on one, he landed on the mainland of America.

After his fourth voyage, the king of Spain put Vespucci in charge of making charts and maps of the new lands being discovered by Spanish explorers.

Vespucci's maps being the best available of the area, the new lands became known as Amerigo land. This name has survived as America.

Sir Walter Raleigh

It has often been said of the reign of Queen Elizabeth I that it was 'A Golden Age'. Certainly it was a period of great adventure; when Sir Francis Drake was sailing round the world, the first Englishman to do so; when other seamen such as Sir Richard Grenville and Sir Martin Frobisher were defying the might of Spain; when great poets like William Shakespeare and Ben Jonson were writing plays and poems that will live forever.

One of the foremost of that band of warriors and poets was Sir Walter Raleigh.

One day, seeing the Queen walking towards a muddy puddle he took off his expensive cloak and threw it down over the puddle so that the Queen did not dirty her shoes. He was one of her favourites for many years.

Raleigh often sailed to America and raided Spanish shipping. He was one of the first to introduce tobacco and potatoes into England. It is said that it was he who named the American colony 'Virginia' in honour of Elizabeth's title 'The Virgin Queen'.

When she died in 1603 James I came to the throne. He imprisoned Raleigh for treason but released him to command an expedition to South America.

On his return from the unsuccessful expedition, Sir Walter Raleigh was tried on the original charge of treason and executed.

Jack Cornwell

Jack Cornwell was one of the youngest ever to win the Victoria Cross, Britain's highest award for valour in battle.

In 1916 Britain was at war with Germany. On May 31st, the German High Seas Fleet was sailing north off Jutland when it was sighted by a small British force under Admiral Beatty. The main British fleet of twenty-four battleships, forty-three cruisers and eighty destroyers was nearby so Beatty turned to join them. One of the rearmost of Beatty's ships was HMS "Chester", a light cruiser.

Sixteen-year-old Jack Cornwell, who had previously served on HMS "Lancaster", was the sightsetter of the "Chester's" forward gun. His job was to adjust the range of the gun to make sure it hit enemy ships. About five o'clock in the afternoon the forward gun was hit by an enemy shell and destroyed. Cornwell was badly wounded but stayed at his post to watch for any change in the direction of the enemy ships.

An hour later the British fleet appeared and Cornwell left his post to receive medical aid. The British had won an important victory. Sadly, Cornwell died a few hours later.

Emmeline Pankhurst

Until 1918 women in Britain were not allowed to vote at elections. The women who protested in favour of being given the vote were led by Emmeline Pankhurst.

She was born in 1858 and in 1879 married a barrister named Dr R. Pankhurst. Ten years later the couple founded the Women's Franchise League which called for women to be given the same voting rights as men. After fourteen years without success, Mrs Pankhurst began the Suffragette movement amid violent demonstrations. She was arrested several times and sent to prison on no less than eight occasions.

In 1914 the First World War began. During the war, women undertook important jobs and made a great contribution to the victory. Finally in 1918 Parliament allowed women to vote at elections.

Mrs Pankhurst had won.

Edith Cavell

During the First World War Edith Cavell became a great heroine in Britain.

When war broke out in 1914 Edith Cavell was the senior nurse at a large hospital in Brussels. When the Germans captured Brussels, she decided to remain.

Early in 1915 an escaped British soldier came to Nurse Cavell and asked for help. She gave him food and a place to rest before he tried to cross the Dutch border and reach freedom. Soon Nurse Cavell was helping many soldiers to escape from the Germans.

On August 5th German secret police arrested her and she was thrown into prison. On October 7th she was tried, found guilty of helping the Germans' enemies and sentenced to death. The American diplomats in Belgium tried to save her life, but the German army insisted. On October 12th Nurse Cavell was executed. Countries not involved in the war were horrified that the Germans should do such a thing.

Yuri Gagarin

The first human being to enter space, Yuri Gagarin became a Hero of the Soviet Union and a world-famous personality.

On April 12th 1961 Yuri Gagarin, aged just twenty-seven, climbed aboard the space craft Vostok 1. The Vostok was perched atop a huge rocket. It consisted of a 2.3 metre sphere packed with scientific instruments and with a tiny seat for the pilot.

A few minutes after take off, Gagarin sent a radio message stating that everything was going as planned. Radio Moscow proudly announced to the world that a man was in space. After a single orbit, lasting just one hundred and eight minutes, Gagarin returned to Earth. He parachuted from his craft before it landed, as planned, for the Soviets had yet to invent a safe landing procedure.

Gagarin was now famous and visited many countries to talk about his mission into space. Gagarin was killed in 1968 when a training mission went tragically wrong.

Marie Curie

Marie Curie was the wife of Pierre Curie and both were brilliant scientists. Pierre studied the effects of heat on magnetism. Marie worked on uranium. Together they discovered radium which is extremely successful in helping to cure many diseases, as well as being of importance in industry.

Their labours were long and arduous. In 1903 they shared the Nobel Prize for Physics. Marie Curie also won a Nobel Prize for Chemistry in 1911.

The Black Prince

Edward, the Black Prince, led the English armies during the Hundred Years War with France. He had a reputation for fierce and brave actions.

He was the eldest son of King Edward III and, because he always wore black armour, he became known as the Black Prince. In 1345, when he was only fifteen years old, his father put him in command of part of the English army at the Battle of Crecy. The small, English army defeated a much larger, French army and Edward fought bravely.

In 1356 Edward led another English army to France. At Poitiers his six thousand men were surprised by a French army of twenty-one thousand. Edward cleverly hid his archers in a vineyard and used his knights to attack the French army. The French were beaten and Edward even managed to capture the French king, John II. In 1362 he was made ruler of those areas of France conquered by England.

In 1371, however, Edward fell ill. He was exhausted with constant campaigning and fighting and died in 1376.